YOUR KNOWLEDGE HAS VALUE

Tze Ping Khor

Keyword Relevance in Search Engine Optimization

GRIN Publishing

Bibliographic information published by the German National Library:

The German National Library lists this publication in the National Bibliography; detailed bibliographic data are available on the Internet at http://dnb.dnb.de .

Imprint:

Copyright © 2014 GRIN Verlag GmbH
Print and binding: Books on Demand GmbH, Norderstedt Germany
ISBN: 978-3-656-70979-4

This book at GRIN:

http://www.grin.com/en/e-book/278141/keyword-relevance-in-search-engine-optimization

GRIN - Your knowledge has value

Since its foundation in 1998, GRIN has specialized in publishing academic texts by students, college teachers and other academics as e-book and printed book. The website www.grin.com is an ideal platform for presenting term papers, final papers, scientific essays, dissertations and specialist books.

Visit us on the internet:

http://www.grin.com/

http://www.facebook.com/grincom

http://www.twitter.com/grin_com

KEYWORD RELEVANCE IN SEARCH ENGINE OPTIMIZATION

KHOR TZE PING

A Master's Project submitted in fulfillment for the requirements for the
degree of Master of Information Technology

Centre of Graduate Studies
Open University Malaysia

2014

Declaration

Name: Khor Tze Ping

I hereby declare that this Master's Project is the result of my own work, except for quotations and summaries which have been duly acknowledged.

Signature: Date:

Abstract

The world of search engines have long been dominated by Google and most internet marketers know that they need to get their websites listed on the first page on Google or risk being totally unseen by their online customers. Almost everyone who is on the internet will search using a search engine for the information they want and rely almost completely on the information given on the first page of the search engine results page. It can be unfortunate for a company which can offer the products its customers want but unfortunately it cannot be found on the first few pages of a search engine retrieved pages. This has created a demand for search engine optimization companies which cater towards individuals and companies hoping to get their website listed on the first page of Google but not knowing how to. The work of search engine optimization is also fraught with errors as search engines like Google keep changing their search algorithms in their quest to perfect their search ability and this means the rules for search engine optimization are always changing too. As content may remain the same it is thus important to be able to find a way to measure the content of a website to determine its relevance for search engines to retrieve a desired webpage. One way to measure the content is to determine the amount of important keywords which make up the content and thus the purpose of this research is to determine the relevance of keywords in today's demanding search technology such as those used by Google and Yahoo. This research also attempts to find out what are the other factors besides keywords which will help a website to rise to the top of a search engine results page.

Keywords: Search engines, search engine optimization, keyword research,

keyword relevance, search engine ranking.

Acknowledgement

I would like to take this opportunity to thank Dr V.P. Thinagaran for his sincere guidance to enable this thesis to be formulated to completion. I would also like to thank the Programme Coordinator Ms Jaspal Kaur for her invaluable help and assistance during the course of my study.

TABLE OF CONTENTS

LIST OF TABLES

LIST OF FIGURES

LIST OF ABBREVIATIONS

DMCA	Digital Millennium Copyright Act
HTML	Hypertext markup language
IP	Internet protocol
SEO	Search engine optimization
SERP	Search engine result page
TLD	Top Level Domains
URI	Uniform resource identifier
URL	Uniform resource locator

CHAPTER 1

1. Introduction

1.1. Background of study

Almost everyone depends on search engines as their first method of searching for information on the internet. Search engines exist for the sole purpose to provide the people who search with the information they want. Many a times the information returned is not relevant or not the intended search material. Search engines have therefore continuously improved to cater for human search behavior to understand the search query and to return the best information available. These days information is so numerous and widespread that search engines have a tough time to determine which is the most relevant information to provide to the searcher. The algorithm used by search engines is important and it is what determines the quality of the search. The algorithm must be able to gauge the intended information requested by the user and to provide the closest results in a descending order so that the closest result will appear first in a Search Engine Result Page (SERP). The user is thereby fully dependent on the search algorithm for the accuracy of the search results shown on the SERP. Since algorithms are closely guarded secrets by the search engines the user actually does not know how the search engine decides what results are to be shown. This research will use one of the search criteria which are called keywords to determine how much it affects the search results by looking at the search results and analyzing the results given by the search engines since not much is known about the algorithms being used. The three major search engines i.e. Google, Yahoo and Bing being the most popular today will be used for this study.

1.2. Objective of study

The objective of this research hereby is to determine how much keywords affect search engine results. This has been a long standing study as keyword relevance in search engines have been debated for a long time on their importance and relevance. It is now known that keyword is just one of the factor search engines look for in a document with the other major factors being the age of the document (search engines presume the older the document the more validity it possess) and the number of inbound links (again, search engines presume the more incoming links or references made towards the document the more authority it possess).

Many people have tried to figure out how search engines work and none more than the so called Search Engine Optimization (SEO) organizations whose work is to figure out for their clients how to make their clients' website appear at the top of SERPs. Obviously there is a real purpose here as everyone wants their website or document to be visible and easily searched and no one wants their hard work to be left unknown by netizens. SEO is also now at the forefront of most marketing campaigns and also on the negative side at the forefront of hackers and marketers of dubious products. Search engines are also aware of this fact and this has made the world of search engines even more complicated as search engines try to omit documents which have dubious content but have made it to the top of SERPs. This method of excluding some websites is of course is never perfect as some valid websites will find themselves being omitted or down ranked by a search engine due to their ever changing rules and algorithms in their quest to improve their search results.

Are keywords the only factor to rank a website?

This research will also be conducted to investigate what are the other factors besides keywords which will affect a search and the ranking of the search results. Factors like link backs, domain age, freshness of content and social media links will also be investigated to see if they affect the overall ranking of a website by a search engine.

1.3. Challenges

There are some challenges towards this research as the results of this study may not accurately reflects the way search engines behave as different search engines have different algorithms and the different geographical locations of a user also affects the way a search engine produces its result due to their geo-targeting behavior. For example a search done on www.google.com and on www.google.com.my will give different results due to geo-targeting as Google tries to provide more Malaysian related websites if a user uses Google.com.my. Due to this, this study will narrow the scope of comparison between websites from the same geographical location.

Another challenge which will affect the results is server redundancies. Since Google and other search engines like Yahoo may have many different servers around the world it is likely that each server may give a slightly different answer due to some differences in their database. In this research resources are limited to control which server is being accessed and slight difference in answers might be possibly due to different servers being accessed during a test.

CHAPTER 2

2. Literature Review

    2.1. Search Engine History

Search engines have come a long way since the first search engine Archie, was invented in 1990 (Kim). Before Google came along and dominated the whole search arena there were many other search engines developed after 1990 which included the likes of InfoSeek, AltaVista, Excite and Yahoo. Google, which was founded by Larry Page and Sergey Brin only came to the fore in 1996 and the rest is history, like they said. As the other search engines drifted into obscurity it is interesting to see that Google remained as strong as ever since its inception. One of the reasons Google differentiated itself from the rest and gained popularity was because of its simplistic design (only text) while the rest cluttered their search page with images and advertisements. Another factor was Google's ingenious implementation of the PageRank factor which ranked websites according to their relevance. PageRank has since seen its importance being played down by Google as its popularity also proved to be its own nemesis when numerous so called SEOs (search optimization organizations) started to multiply in masses to take advantage of Google's PageRank technology to tweak certain websites to make them appear at the top of Google's search listing, thereby making Google's search results seem manipulated.

2.2. Popularity vs. Relevancy

In the world of search engines popularity and relevancy of a website are two different things. A site may be popular but may not be relevant for a search. Conversely, a site may be relevant for a search but may not be that popular.

Popularity is determined by the number of links pointing towards a site. The more links pointing towards a site the more popular it is (Dover & Dafforn, 2011). Since popularity of a site does not mean it is relevant to a search, another metric to gauge relevancy has to be determined. Think of it as a site like Facebook. Facebook is a site which is very popular and may turn up in your searches but it does not mean a search like "buy Christmas stockings" should end up in Facebook as Facebook does not sell Christmas stockings.

In the world of search engines, relevancy is determined by the theoretical distance between two corresponding items with regards to relationship (Dover & Dafforn, 2011). Search engines therefore need to determine relevancy by analyzing the content of a webpage, website or document. A webpage with more relevant content would be ranked higher than a webpage with less relevant content. This would enable the search engine to use a list based on the rankings to present the search results to the searcher with the highest ranked webpage being shown first and followed by the other webpages with lower ranks in succession.

2.3. How Does A Web Search Works

To search for a document rapidly, computers uses a full-text index, whereby the list of all the words appear in a text together with a pointer to every occurrence (Witten, Gori, & Numerico, 2007). The size of the list of pointers will depend on how many times a word reoccur in a document. The index will contain as many words as there are in the text of the document. The size of the index will be about the size of the document and the size of the list of pointers will be much smaller. However both the sizes of the index and list of pointers can still be compressed. Search engines will therefore store both the document and the full-text index in their database.

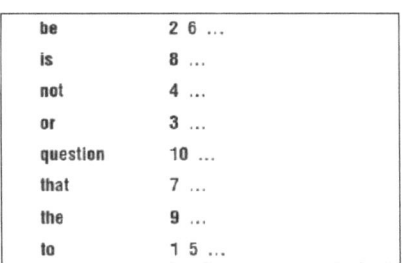

(a) The beginning of the index.

(b) The text.

Figure 2.1 Creating a full-text index (Witten et al., 2007)

Once the index is available a search can then be performed by just locating the ordered list and extracting its associated list of numbers. A search will then be able to find all the documents that contain the particular word being searched. Once an ordered list has been created it will be easy and fast for a computer to scan through them. To search for a phrase the computer will perform a proximity search whereas words which occur near to each other are selected.

2.4. Accuracy of Search Engines

To determine if the results of a search are relevant to a query a computer must decide on the following (Witten et al., 2007):

A document will be deemed more relevant:

- If it contains more query terms
- If the query terms occur more often
- If it contains fewer non-query terms

A good indexing system will answer queries quickly and effectively, be able to rebuild new indexes and do not require large resources, all of which are easily done with the present computing power available. The difficult part is to determine the effectiveness of the answer or the relevance of the search result. The most common way to measure the relevance of a search result is to calculate **how many** of the relevant documents have been retrieved and **how early** they occur in the ranked list.

Retrieval performance is measured by three quantities:

- The number of documents that are retrieved
- The number of those that are relevant
- The total number of relevant documents

The factor for *precision* and *recall* are then calculated as follows:

$$Precision = \frac{Number\ of\ retrieved\ documents\ that\ are\ relevant}{Total\ number\ retrieved}$$

$$Recall = \frac{Number\ of\ relevant\ documents\ that\ are\ relevant}{Total\ number\ relevant}$$

Precision assesses the accuracy of the search in terms of what proportion are good results while *recall* indicates the coverage of what proportion of good results are returned.

As an example, if 20 documents are retrieved and 15 of them are relevant this would give a *precision* of 75%. If the collection contains 60 relevant documents in total then the *recall* would be 25%.

The world of search engines has been made a lot challenging due to the millions of documents being added to the web almost daily. Search engines need to do their work accurately and at a fast speed to prove that they are worthy to be used.

2.5. Calculating PageRank

As search engines start to become more efficient there were other human factors which start to crop up as if there were not enough problems for search engines. When people started to realize that search engines were measuring often occurring keywords (words which are key to a document), they knew that if they put in more keywords in a document this would make the document easier to find. Hence a person selling cars for example can easily get his website noticed more than for example BMW or Toyota if he puts in more keywords in his website as compared to BMW or Toyota. This presented a new problem to search engines to determine a website's relevance and one solution to overcome this problem was to create a measurement factor called the PageRank (Witten et al., 2007) .

A website is deemed to be more important or relevant if there are other websites or documents pointing back to that website or using it as a reference. However, if two websites both having exactly 20 other websites pointing back to it how do you determine which is more relevant? Google's founders Larry Page and Sergey Brin developed a metric called the PageRank in 1998 which was able to measure a website's importance by measuring the link backs or backlinks to a website (Witten et al., 2007).

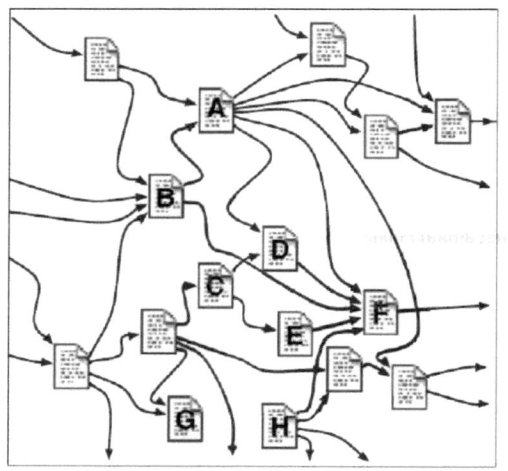

Figure 2.2 Measuring PageRank (Witten et al., 2007)

The PageRank of a page is a number from 0 to 1 which measures the importance of backlinks towards that website or webpage. Each link towards the page contributes a factor towards its overall PageRank number. That factor is determined by the PageRank of the referring site divided by the number of outlinks (the total number of links going out) from that site. Obviously it is more prestigious for a site to have inbound links rather than outbound links and this is what PageRank aims to measure.

As an example, in Figure 2.2, the PageRank of D can be calculated by adding one-fifth of the value of the PageRank of A (since it has five outlinks) with one-half of the value of the PageRank of C (since it has two outlinks). By using the PageRank method almost every website can be allotted a PageRank number and a higher PageRank number will add towards its importance of being ranked higher compared to other websites with lower PageRank numbers.

2.6. Importance of Keywords

Different search engines use different methods and algorithms to determine the relevance of documents in order to list them in their order of their importance or relevance when a user performs a search. Needless to say Google has managed to secure the majority of users by implementing its PageRank approach to the extent of other search engines trying to copy their algorithms and leading also to the death of many of the earlier search engines which could not match Google's accuracy and speed.

However, PageRank is not the only sole factor Google and other search engine uses and there are many other factors which can determine a document's relevance and importance.

On the search term itself a search engine will determine if the word being searched appears in document constantly and where it occurs e.g. (Witten et al., 2007) :

- The anchor text
- The title
- The URL (universal resource locator)
- Headings
- The meta tags

Each search engine will employ its own algorithm to determine the overall importance of the page in terms of the occurrence and location of the searched word or term and no one knows precisely what algorithm will be used by individual search engines. Furthermore the search algorithm used by Google, for example, changes regularly as Google attempts to improve their search engine's results and relevance (Sullivan, Sep 26, 2013).

It was believed in the past that search engines liked to see keywords in certain locations of the HTML code to help indicate a page's relevance for that query. Nowadays, this is not very true anymore as relevancy and keyword-based algorithms that Google and Bing use to evaluate and rank pages are massively more complex now. Gaining a slight benefit in a keyword placement-based algorithmic element may even actually harm overall rankings because of how it impacts people's experience with your site (Fishkin, 2013).

In a recent survey conducted on 130 SEO professionals in 2013 (Fishkin, 2013), the ranking factors that matters most to the professionals were queried and the results are shown as in Figure 2.3.

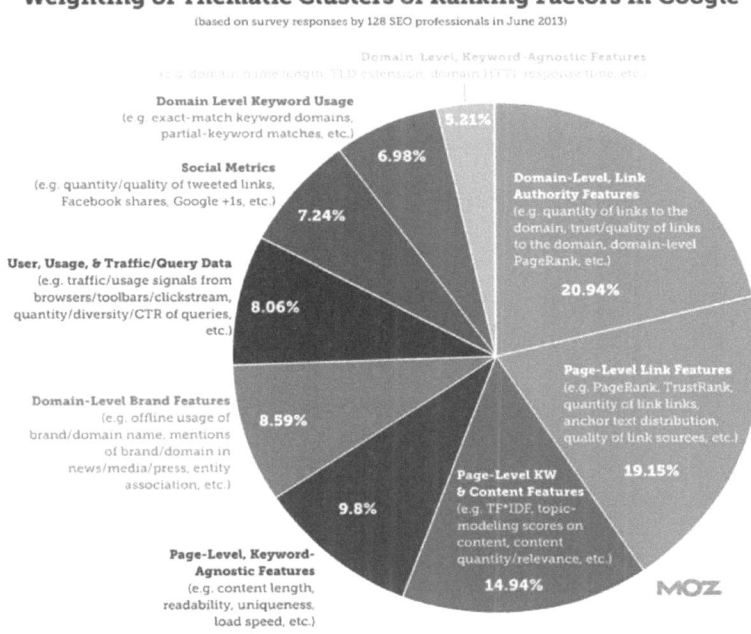

Figure 2.3 Weighting of Keywords in Ranking (Fishkin, 2013)

In this survey it was found that less than fifteen percent in the rankings equation actually involved keyword targeting. Although most of the professionals surveyed believed keywords are not that important anymore in the overall ranking it cannot be denied that keywords still plays a role in search engine rankings.

Search engines are now not just looking for a page filled with keywords but are more interested in an "optimized" page. Basically an optimized page is one that must provide unique content and value. Search engines are more intelligent now and they seek this unique value where social shares, links, all the other positive associations and branding come together to create all the right signals to propel the website to the top (Fishkin, 2013).

At the very basic level, an optimized page is one that is:

- Easy to understand
- Providing intuitive navigation and content consumption
- Loading quickly, even on slower connections (like mobile)
- Rendering properly in any browser size and on any device
- Designed to be visually attractive/pleasing/compelling

While search engines are getting more intelligent, it remains a fact that they are still using automated bots or crawlers to look for signs of an optimized page which will provide the visitor with a good user experience. As bots being what they are it is important to provide all the necessary help to these bots to enable them to crawl a website for the information you want it to find.

All the important information in a website has to be properly located and especially the keywords need to be located in the following areas:

- Page title
- Headline
- Body text

- URL
- Image and image ALT attributes
- Internal and external links
- Meta description
- Meta keywords

The above are the locations where bots will expect to find the keywords to enable a search engine to rank a website based on the keywords used (Fishkin, 2013).

Since it is a known fact that bots are used to read keywords there are people who will resort to keyword stuffing or to use a lot of keywords in the hope that bots will rank their sites higher. Although this was done in the past search engines are now smarter and this is one reason why keyword count are no longer the major factor in ranking a website. There are also ways to measure keyword relevance where the use of particular keywords are judged to see if they have been used excessively. Google has been known to penalize websites that used keywords excessively or those which try to hide their keywords from view but are still inserted as codes for the bots to read.

As keywords are being less relied on for search rankings it is also important to note if the other search engines besides Google are also placing less reliance on keywords for ranking. It must be remembered that most search engines in the past placed a lot of importance on keywords and their viability depended on how well they were able to please search engine users with the search results.

2.7. How Do Search Engines Remain Viable

As most search engines employ their own custom designed algorithms to run their search engine, these algorithms are highly secretive and remain as corporate secrets to protect the business viability. Search engines like Google earn from advertising which are discreetly inserted into search engine results pages or SERPs. If a user cannot find the information he wants, search engines presume that the user might click on one of the ads which will be presented to him on the same page. It is indeed a paradox as to whether the search engines prefer their user to find the information he wants or to click on one of the ads (in the event that he did not find suitable information) which will then add revenue into the search engine's operational profit.

Until Google's appearance in 1998, search engines followed the classic model of information retrieval: to see if a document is a good match to its query, you only need to look inside the document itself. Google changed all that with the introduction of PageRank then and created an earthquake in the world of search engines which left few survivors in its wake. In 2005 only five major search engines remain: Google, Yahoo, MSN Search, AOL and Ask (Witten et al., 2007). In 2013, the landscape has remained without much changes with Google, Bing (Microsoft), Yahoo, Ask and AOL in the order of preference as rated by comScore and with Google taking up almost 67% percent of market share in terms of search ("comScore Releases July 2013 U.S. Search Engine Rankings,").

Table 2.1 comScore Search Share Report for July 2013 ("comScore Releases July 2013 U.S. Search Engine Rankings,")

Core Search Entity	Explicit Core Search Share (%)
Google	67.0
Bing (Microsoft)	17.9
Yahoo	11.3
Ask	2.7
AOL	1.2

2.8. What is Search Engine Optimization (SEO)?

The term Search Engine Optimization (SEO) can be used to describe a diverse set of activities that can be performed to increase the number of desired visitors to a website via search engines (Couzin et al., 2008). These include actions such as making changes to the text and HTML code, communicating directly with the search engines and pursuing other sources of traffic for listings or links. SEO is basically doing things to set up a website so that it ranks well for particular keywords that visitors will search for in search engines. Unlike paid search marketing which requires you to pay for every click sent to your website, SEO is about getting traffic sent to your site from the search engine's organic results for free (Jones, 2008).

SEO started in 1997 through public reports and commentaries provided by search engine experts such as Danny Sullivan and Bruce Clay, among others (Jones, 2008). Early reports about SEO looked at search engine algorithms and how the various search engines ranked search results. Inspired entrepreneurs and website owners began studying these reports and tested strategies on how they could rank well on the search results. Inevitably, it soon became a business and a profession for some to be engaged in the services to provide SEO advice and help to others to help them achieve better rankings for their websites.

As the World Wide Web grew at a remarkable pace the popularity of some search engines like Alta Vista and Infoseek started to diminish while Google which was incorporated in 1998 became stronger and bigger. Google's early success was due to their ground breaking new algorithm which made use of their proprietary PageRank formula and also the fact that their web interface was less clustered with advertisements. Google today is much more complex and they have grown to be the leading search engine with over 60 percent in market share (Jones, 2008). This has invariably made them the target for almost every SEO companies out there as they (SEO companies) know that everyone wants to get their website listed on Google to attract as much traffic as possible from organic search.

Although there are also many who practiced SEO unethically to obtain traffic to their websites it cannot be denied that SEO is a much sought after service nowadays as many companies do not have the time to ensure that their website will be well ranked as they may not be familiar as to what the various search engines are looking for. Also most website creators are naturally more concerned about the content and design they put inside their webpages rather than thinking about whether their content or design will be "liked" by the search engines.

As a website developer though it cannot be denied that SEO is important as very few developers actually develop websites where traffic or visitors are not wanted. If you are looking for visitors and lots of it then you will have to pay heed to what

18

SEO is all about or risk being sidelined by the search engines as there are possibly thousands of other similar websites as yours and search engine visitors hardly look past the first few pages of the search results. Therefore, since Google is the favored search engine of the day it definitely does not pay to not understand how Google works if it is traffic you are looking for.

2.9. How Does Google Work?

Since Google is now the preferred search engine it will be used as the search engine for study. Google goes through a few basic steps to index a website before someone can search the website from its huge database.

The basic steps taken by Google are as follows ("How Does Google Collect and Rank Results," 10 January 2006):

- A webmaster can submit his website URL to Google for it to be indexed by Google's robot or wait until the robot trawls the whole internet and stumble upon the website which of course will take a long time.

- After indexing the site the robot will read the contents of the website and store relevant information like keywords into its database. The keywords are important because it will help the robot to find back the same document if someone searches for a document with that keyword. Also the frequency of the keyword in the document or the whole domain will also be measured to ascertain how important or relevant the keyword is as used in the actual search term.

- Keywords are not the only deciding factor for Google to retrieve a document during a search as Google also need to determine how important is the document and this is where their search algorithm goes into full gear. To rank a document in terms of relevance Google uses their proprietary PageRank algorithm to determine how many links are there which point back towards the document or the so called number of backlinks. The more links there are the better the PageRank, but the PageRank algorithm is much more sophisticated as it also measures the "quality" of the backlink i.e. where is the link coming from, is it from a reputable site e.g. *CNN.com*?

- Google today has progressed to more than just using PageRank to determine a website's relevance and in its latest incarnation – "Hummingbird", Google reveals that PageRank is just one of over 200 other major ingredients that go into Hummingbird. (Sullivan, Sep 26, 2013). The other factors Google now measures are divided into the following groups as presented on Table 2.2. ("The Periodic Table Of SEO Success Factors,")

Table 2.2 Periodic Table of SEO Success Factors ("The Periodic Table Of SEO Success Factors,")

CONTENT	HTML	ARCHITECTURE	LINKS	TRUST	SOCIAL	PERSONAL
Quality	Titles	Crawler	Quality	Authority	Reputation	Country
Research	Description	Duplicate	Text	History	Shares	Locality
Words	Headers	Speed	Backlinks	Identity		History
Engaging	Structured Data	Meaningful URLs	Paid Links	Piracy		Social
Fresh	Keyword Stuffing	Mobile	Spam			
Thin Content	Hidden Text	Cloaking				
Ads Heavy						

20

Search Engine Land (www.searchengineland.com) sees Google as now using a group of factors to identify a website's popularity and relevance to correctly rank it in its SERP when a user requests for particular information.

In the Periodic Table of SEO Success Factors ("The Periodic Table of SEO Success Factors,") the writers of Search Engine Land propounded that there are three main groups of factors affecting search engine rankings and more sub-groups within the three main groups. The three main groups are:

- On The Page SEO
- Off The Page SEO
- Violations

There is no one particular factor affecting search engine ranking and a combination of the correct factors will raise the rankings of a website. On The Page search ranking factors are those that are entirely within the publisher's own control e.g. the HTML code and architecture. Off The Page ranking factors are those that publishers do not directly control like links to the website, social media links and trustworthiness of the publisher. Violations are mainly tactics used to deceive or manipulate a search engine's understanding of a site's true relevancy and authority and will actually bring down the ranking of the website.

Explanation on the SEO success factors:

(i) On The Page SEO

    (a) Content

        Quality – Are pages well written and have quality content?

        Research – Have the keywords been properly researched?

        Words – Are words and phrases used as what they will be searched for?

        Engage – How long does a visitor spend time on that page?

        Fresh – Are pages "fresh" and about "hot" topics?

    (b) HTML

        Titles – Do title tags contain keywords relevant to topics?

        Description – Do meta tags describe the page properly?

        Headers – Are headlines/headers using relevant keywords?

        Structure – Do pages use structured data?

    (c) Architecture

        Crawl – Can search engines easily "crawl" the site?

        Duplicate – Are there duplicate content in the site?

        Speed – Does site load quickly?

        URL – Are URLs short and meaningful?

        Mobile – Does the site work well for mobile?

(ii) Off The Page SEO

    (a) Links

        Quality – Are links from trusted and respectable sites?

        Text – Do links pointing at pages use word you hope they will be found?

        Number – Do many links point at your web pages?

(b) Trust

     Authority – Do links and shares make site a trusted authority?

     History – Has site or domain been around for a long time?

     Identity – Does site use means to verify identity of its authors?

(c) Social

     Reputation – Do those respected on social networks share your content?

     Shares – Do many share your content on social networks?

(d) Personal

     Country - What country is someone located in?

     Locality – What city or local area is someone located in?

     History – Has someone regularly visited the site?

     Social – Has someone socially favored the site?

(iii)   Violations

    (a) Thin or Shallow Content

    (b) Ads / Top Heavy Layout

    (c) Keywords Stuffing

    (d) Hidden Text

    (e) Cloaking

    (f) Paid Links

    (g) Link Spam

    (h) Piracy / DMCA Takedowns

Each of the above 33 factors will either contribute towards (blue/unshaded) or pull down (red/shaded) a website's ranking in Google. Search Engine Land understands that there are 200 main factors in Google's algorithm (Google is not telling which are the 200) and believes that their 33 factors is a good approximation of the algorithm Google is using (Sullivan, Sep 17, 2010).

2.10. Related Research

Geetha, S. and Sathiyakumari, K. has done research on the prediction model for page ranking of blogs (Geetha & Sathiyakumari, 2012) by studying the effects of link backs, social network links and data structure on a page being ranked by search engines. Geetha and Sathiyakumari used MozRank (http://moz.com/learn/seo/mozrank) as one of their tools in their research to determine the popularity of a domain to gauge the effect of popularity on a page ranking. MozRank which is now being incorporated inside Open Site Explorer (http://www.opensiteexplorer.org/) will also be used in this author's research. Using the Open Site Explorer the user is able to determine the following important metrics which are used to rank a website:

i.   Page Authority – which is based on an algorithmic combination of all link metrics to predict a page's rank potential.

ii. Domain Authority – which is based on an algorithmic combination of all metrics to predict a domain's ranking potential.

iii. Linking Authority – which is the number of unique root domains containing at least one link to the URL

iv. Total Links – which is the number of all links to the URL including internal, external, followed and not followed.

24

In their research, Geetha, S. and Sathiyakumari, K. found that Open Site Explorer was useful as it enables the user to compare up to five URLs at the same time to compare the metrics being measured.

Sharma, D.K. and Sharma, A.K. has also done research to compare the different algorithms being used to rank a webpage and to study the various parameters affecting a search engine ranking (Sharma & Sharma, 2010). The purpose of their research was to analyze the current algorithms used for ranking web pages to find their relative strength and limitations in order to find ways to improve the ranking of web pages. The algorithms they analyzed were the

    i.   Page Rank algorithm

    ii.   HITS algorithm,

    iii.   Weighted Page algorithm,

    iv.   Weighted Links Rank algorithm,

    v.   EigenRumor algorithm,

    vi.   Distance Rank algorithm,

    vii.   Time Rank algorithm,

    viii.   TagRank algorithm,

    ix.   Relation Based algorithm,

    x.   Query Dependent Ranking algorithm,

    xi.   Ranking and Suggestive algorithm,

    xii.   Comparison and Score Based algorithm

    xiii.   Algorithm for Query Processing in Uncertain Databases

    xiv.   Ranking of Journal based on Page Rank and HITS algorithm

Based on their research it was found that content, back links and keywords were the main parameters that were observed to provide relevancy in a search although it was not conclusive if there were other factors that were also affecting the search results.

Shika Goel and Sunita Yadav did a research on search engine evaluation based on page level keywords (Goel, 2013) and used the keyword count to judge the performance of the three search engines namely Google, Bing and Yahoo on educational queries. Page level keywords are keywords found on the individual pages of a website such as in the title, header tags, anchor text, meta tags, ALT tags, in the URL string and finally in the content.

Based on their findings that page level keywords are one of the most critical factors in determining search engine ranking, they did a research by using various queries submitted to the three search engines and created a database for the results. The page level keywords were then calculated from the search results from forty educational queries randomly selected from a set of most searched queries. Only keywords (one word) were used instead of phrases for their method and the top ten pages retrieved from each search engine was then saved in a page repository.

The pages retrieved were then parsed to match the input keyword and the total keywords and the average keyword count were then calculated. The average keyword count for the first ten pages was then used to score for the search engine.

Their results showed that Yahoo is ranking websites based on keywords considerably higher followed by Bing and Google respectively. Goel and Yadav also found that Yahoo showed more interest in keywords present in the title tag rather than in the content and used it as the biggest ranking factor to rank web pages. To verify their results the researchers also used human ranking to determine the number of relevant pages by using a precision measurement where the number of relevant results were divided by 10 and then calculated for the forty keywords tested. The human ranking results showed similar trends whereby Yahoo was measured as the most relevant and Google the least as shown in Table 2.3.

Table 2.3 Page Level Average Keyword Count (Goel, 2013)

S.No.	Search Engines	Page Level Average Keyword Count	Mean Average Precision
1	Google	528.75	0.43
2	Yahoo	915.725	0.51
3	Bing	875.45	0.49

Based on their research Goel and Yadav concluded that Yahoo provided the most relevant results based on the educational keywords submitted but it must be pointed out here that relevance based on keywords alone is again very subjective to interpretations (more so when done by human ranking). As it is, many search engines nowadays do not depend on keywords alone to measure the relevancy of their results.

Dania Bilal (Bilal, 2012) did a research in 2012 to evaluate Google, Yahoo, Bing, Yahoo Kids and Ask Kids on their retrieval performance for queries related to children. Two categories of research questions were addressed in his study: (a) benchmarking retrieved hits and their ranking positions and (b) judging relevancy of hits to calculate recall and precision. To address these, two quantitative research designs were employed to answer the research questions: (a) benchmarking ranked output by the search engines and (b) intellectual relevance judgment. The purpose of Bilal doing his research on information retrieval for children was to gain insight into the performance of the search engines he was studying by reducing the complexities of an otherwise adult search environment.

To calculate recall and precision Bilal used a variation of the precision metric that focused on the first results page with a cutoff at 10 hits per page.

For the first method, Bilal selected Google as a benchmark since it was the leading search engine to compare the results from the other four search engines.

Two sets of queries were formulated for the research. In the first set, a corpus of 130 queries were extracted from studying children's queries over a period of time and covers different topic domains (e.g. medicine, health, history and social studies). The second set of 25 queries was compiled by a graduate student from studying children in a middle school library. Fifteen unique queries were then selected from the first set and included 5 one-word, 5 two-words and 5 phases or natural language queries. Similarly, 15 unique queries were also selected from the second set giving a total of 30 queries overall.

Each query from the first set was then submitted to a given search engine and the first results page was recorded for analysis on January 31, 2011 between 10.00

pm and 11.15 pm to avoid any possible changes in results due to search engine updates. The second set was similarly submitted on April 18, 2011 between 9.05 and 11.07 pm from the same geographical location. The total submissions resulted in 150 first page results for the five search engines and since the first ten results were recorded a total of 1,500 results were then made available for the study. From the 1,500 results 140 were found to be broken links and were then removed leaving a total of 1,360 results that were judged.

From the 1,360 hits calculation was done for precision and recall including total precision (TP) and average precision (AP). Since Google was used as a benchmark, retrieved hits from Yahoo, Bing, Yahoo Kids and Ask Kids were compared with the top five hits from Google and the overlap in hits were calculated.

For the one-word query cluster it was found that 44% of Yahoo's results had the same ranking as Google, 28.3% from Bing was similar, 18.7% from Ask Kids was similar and 0% from Yahoo Kids.

For the two-word query cluster it was found that 30% of Yahoo's results had the same ranking as Google, 24% from Bing was similar, 33% from Yahoo Kids was similar and 22% from Ask Kids was similar.

Finally, for the natural language query cluster it was found that 8% of Yahoo's results had the same ranking as Google, 20% from Bing was similar, 0% from Yahoo Kids was similar and 37.5% from Ask Kids was similar.

In summary, the results showed that the engines retrieved a higher percentage in hit overlaps that matched Google's top five hits on the one-word queries (35.7%), followed by two-word queries (26.7%) and natural language queries (16.4%) as shown on Table 2.4.

Table 2.4 Summary of ranking and hit overlap by the engines (Bilal, 2012)

Query Cluster	Google as a benchmark All query clusters (n=30)		
	Hits with same ranking positions as Google Top 5	Overlap with Google	%
One-word	30	84	35.7
Two-word	19	71	26.7
Phrase/natural language	10	61	16.4

Bilal concluded that the hits overlap by the engines and their ranking positions against a benchmark did not provide a deep understanding of the retrieval performance of the engines and therefore intellectual relevance judgment was employed as a second method to measure this performance based on recall and precision metrics. Relevance judgments of retrieved output on the submitted queries produced by the search engines were evaluated by the jurors.

In his second study, retrieval output from the five search engines on children's queries was judged by him and a trained assistant based on "topicality" of the retrieved titles of links, summaries and documents against the context for which children formulated their queries. Besides "topicality", "utility" which was based on the two jurors' interpretation of the contribution of the retrieved hits was also used to fulfill the requirements of relevance in the search results. Bilal also used the ranking positions of hits on the first results page as a key factor in evaluating the engines.

Graded relevance with a 3-point scale was used to judge relevancy of the retrieved hits (1 = *relevant*, 0.5 = *partially relevant*, 0 = *not relevant*). Retrieved hits relevant to one or more of the components of an open-ended query were judged as "partially relevant" instead of "not relevant".

The results from the first results page were used with a cut-off of 10 hits per page. Similar as to the first method, 2 sets of queries, each with 5 one-word, 5 two-words and 5 natural language queries were submitted to the five search engines. Precision of the hits were calculated using a P@10 metric for the 1,360 search results recorded of which 655 were found relevant (P = 0.48), 386 were found partially relevant (P = 0.28) and nearly 24% of the hits were found not relevant.

From the overall results, Google was found to have 163 relevant results out of 296 output (P = 0.55), 85 partially relevant results (P = 0.28) and 48 non-relevant results.

Yahoo was found to have 163 relevant results out of 289 output (P = 0.56), 87 partially relevant results (P = 0.30) and 39 non-relevant results.

Bing was found to have 166 relevant results out of 289 output (P = 0.57), 83 partially relevant results (P = 0.28) and 40 non-relevant results.

Yahoo Kids was found to have 48 relevant results out of 226 output (P = 0.21), 59 partially relevant results (P = 0.26) and 119 non-relevant results.

Ask Kids was found to have 115 relevant results out of 260 output (P = 0.44), 75 partially relevant results (P = 0.29) and 70 non-relevant results.

The summary of the results are shown in Table 2.5.

Table 2.5 Summary of relevancy and precision by search engine (Bilal, 2012)

Engine	Relevance	No. of hits	P+	%
Google (output = 296)	Relevant	163	0.55	
	Partially relevant	85	0.29	
	Not relevant	48		16.22
Yahoo! (output = 289)	Relevant	163	0.56	
	Partially relevant	87	0.30	
	Not relevant	39	–	14.49
Bing (output = 289)	Relevant	166	0.57	
	Partially relevant	83	0.29	
	Not relevant	40	–	13.84
Yahoo! Kids (output = 226)	Relevant	48	0.21	
	Partially relevant	59	0.26	
	Not relevant	119	–	52.65
Ask Kids (output = 260)	Relevant	115	0.44	
	Partially relevant	75	0.29	
	Not relevant	70	–	26.92

The precision that the engines produced for the different types of clusters (one word, two words and natural language) were found to be varied.

For one-word queries, Bing produced the highest precision ratio (P = 0.45), followed by Yahoo (P = 0.42), Google (P = 0.36), Ask Kids (P = 0.36) and Yahoo Kids (P = 0.17).

For two-word queries, Bing again produced the highest precision ratio (P = 0.69), followed by Yahoo (P = 0.66), Ask Kids (P = 0.61), Google (P = 0.60) and Yahoo Kids (P = 0.34).

For natural language queries, Google outperforms the others with the highest precision ratio (P = 0.69), followed by Yahoo (P = 0.61), Bing (P = 0.59), Ask Kids (P = 0.34), and Yahoo Kids (P = 0.13).

Average Precision (AP) calculated for relevant and partially relevant hits by the five engines across all the clusters showed that they were most effective for the two-word query cluster (AP = 0.59), followed by natural language queries (AP = 0.49) and finally one-word queries (AP = 0.36). This is shown again in Table 2.6.

Total Precision (TP) which took into account of both relevant and partially relevant hits calculated showed that Bing produced the highest TP ratio (0.83), followed by Yahoo (0.83), Google (0.74), Ask Kids (0.73) and Yahoo Kids (0.47).

Table 2.6 Average precision (AP) across query clusters (Bilal, 2012)

One-word	AP	Two-word	AP	Phrase	AP
Relevant	0.36	Relevant	0.59	Relevant	0.49
Partially relevant	0.38	Partially relevant	0.22	Partially relevant	0.26

Based on this research by Bilal, this author's research will be conducted on two-word queries as it was found to have the best average precision. Also Google, Bing and Yahoo will be selected as the main search engines to study based on Bilal's research that Google produced the highest precision ratio for natural language (phrase) queries while Bing and Yahoo produced the highest and second highest total precision scores respectively.

2.11. Research Questions

Based on the literature survey and related past research, the objective of this study will be to obtain a better understanding on whether keywords are a still a main factor in ranking websites by search engines. The specific questions to be addressed are as follows:

1. Are search engine ranking websites based on number of keywords?
2. Are link backs also being used to rank by search engines?
3. Are domain age and freshness of site being used to rank?
4. Are social network links being used to rank?

2.12. Research Limitations

Due to limitation of resources such as testing from various geographical locations and the time needed to collect and study a large collection of keywords, this research will try to study the effect of these factors especially keywords in the overall rank of a website by comparing results from the different search engines.

Another factor which might affect the tests is server redundancies whereby different servers located worldwide might store slightly different versions of the internet and there is no way to control which server is being accessed during a test. This will affect the results as different servers might give different results for a same test. Due to limitations of resources test will be conducted from a single location although this does not guarantee that it will not be affected by server redundancies.

It is possible some results might also be affected by search engines performing geo-targeting to bring more geographically correct results to the user based on his location. Google, for example, shows different search results for different computers based on the IP address of the computer (Agarwal, 2007). So if a search is done on Google.com, Google will try to determine the location of the user from his IP address and retrieve results relevant towards the user's location. This invariably will cause some differences in the result for different users with different IPs and it may cause some problems for research if one is not sure which IP is one using especially for users with assigned IPs. Using Google's local search engine (e.g. Google.com.my) might reduce the variances as Google will then assume the user is searching from Malaysia or for information relevant for Malaysia. However the resolution of how Google is able to determine a user's exact location and its accuracy may further cause changes to its result and the effect is beyond the scope of this research.

A recent research done by Linkdex found high level of variance for 2000 keywords tested across 10 major US cities in 2012 (Miller, 2012) as shown in Figure 2.4.

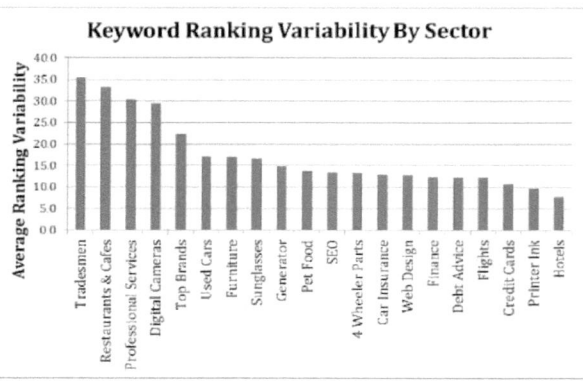

Figure 2.4 Variance due to geo-targeting (Miller, 2012)

Linkdex found that in 69 percent of cases where a company's website ranks in the top 30 on Google for one location, it doesn't rank for that keyword across all other locations. They also studied the ranking variations across 10 different geo-locations and found that ranking deviated by an average of 11 positions for the different locations.

This research will try to detect and avoid geo-targeting or geo-location by the search engines since the results can be affected or skewed if a certain search engine that uses geo-targeting is compared with another which does not employ geo-targeting.

CHAPTER 3

3. Research Methodology

    3.1. Test Platform

To perform the analysis a test platform will be created with a loose framework to reduce the time it takes to conduct the tests and to enable the tests to be manipulated and easily monitored. A benchmark website will be created and available online analysis tools will be selected to test the benchmark website and other websites. The tests done will also be highly customizable since the controlled benchmark website will be used to test the results.

    3.2. Benchmark Website Creation

A controlled website has been created not wholly for test and experiment but a real life website with real functionalities. This website was also submitted to the major search engines for indexing and a good measure of time (e.g. at least a year) was given for the search engines to properly index the site. This is to ensure that all the search engines targeted are on an equal footing for the experiments conducted on this website. Also using a controlled website enables checks with available search engine management (analytics) programs to verify that certain tools being used are accurate for the tests. The importance here is to benchmark the rankings using sites that have already been indexed by the search engines using available tools online and offline.

3.3. Keywords Creation

The controlled website created has a few known keywords which will be chosen for the experiments. These keywords were chosen on the basis that they are not very common keywords for search as to narrow down the number of results gathered by the search engines.

3.4. Keywords Counting

The number of keywords in each page is determined by various available online applications and a reliable application is chosen. The exact number of keywords on each test page will be recorded.

A free keyword density tool from the SEO Book (http://www.seobook.com) will be used to calculate the keywords for the sites to be tested as shown in Figure 3.1. The keywords location in title, meta tags and in text will be noted.

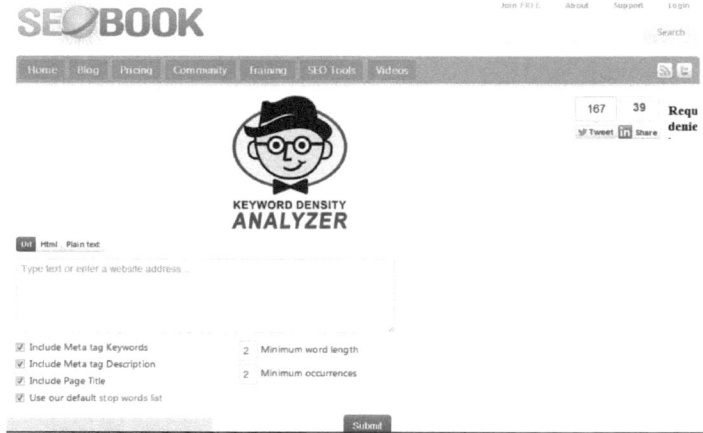

Figure 3.1 Keyword Density Tool

In this research only keyword count was taken into account and not keyword density as recent studies (Anderson, 2009) have shown that keyword density does not affect a site's ranking and might even contribute negatively towards the ranking.

3.5. Search Engine Ranking Check

The exact term of phrase using the keywords will be submitted for search on our targeted search engines and the rank or placement of the webpage will be recorded.

A free rank checking tool from SEO Centro (http://www.seocentro.com) will be used to check the rank of sites to be tested on the three search engines namely Google, Yahoo and Bing as shown in Figure 3.2.

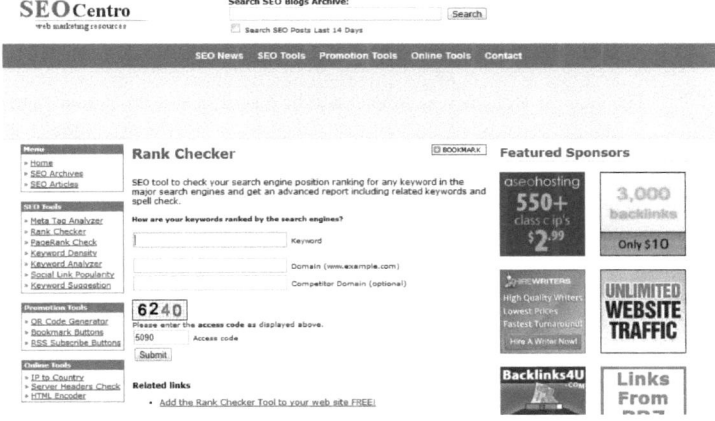

Figure 3.2 Rank Checking Tool

3.6. Inbound Links Check

The number of inbound links or also known as backlinks to each page will be calculated and tabulated. A free tool from ahrefs (http://ahrefs.com) will be used as shown in Figure 3.3.

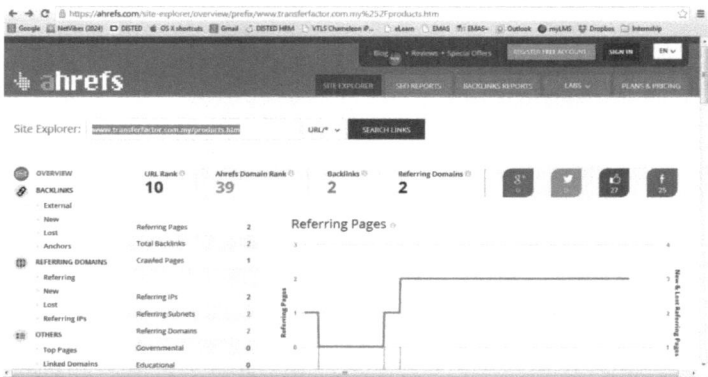

Figure 3.3 Backlinks Check Tool

3.7. Analysis of Domain Age

The year the website was created will be determined using domain age analysis. A free domain age checking tool from SEOChat (http://www.seochat.com) will be used as shown in Figure 3.4.

Figure 3.4 Domain Age Checking Tool

3.8. Analysis of Recent Updates.

A check will be made on the freshness of the website i.e. how recent was the website updated.

A free tool from Sitebeam (http://www.sitebeam.net) was used to check how up-to-date the tested site is, as shown in Figure 3.5.

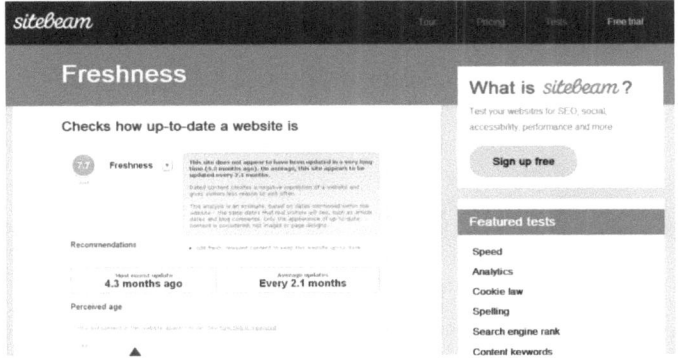

Figure 3.5 Site Freshness Tool

41

3.9. Analysis of Social Interest

As Google is now ranking their results using social interest as a ranking factor ("The Periodic Table Of SEO Success Factors,"), SiteBeam (http://www.sitebeam.net/) will also be used to measure the social interest score for websites to see if social interest is also affecting the ranking of search engines, as shown in Figure 3.6. The number of links from Facebook and Twitter are measured and an overall score is given.

Figure 3.6 Social Interest Check Tool

3.10   Overall Analysis

The tests will be done on selected keywords which will be used to submit to the top three search engines namely Google, Bing and Yahoo. A few websites will be selected from the search results based on similar location and domain levels to avoid geo-location being a factor of the search. The ranking of a website will be recorded and the number of keywords will be counted based on the search. The other search metrics e.g. backlinks, freshness, domain age and social interest will also be measured and used as a reference if it is found that keywords alone cannot determine the results of a search.

After the first test is concluded different keywords will be used and a new search is conducted on all three search engines to narrow down the factors which are affecting the results of a search. Subsequent tests will then be done until a conclusion can be made as shown in Figure 3.7.

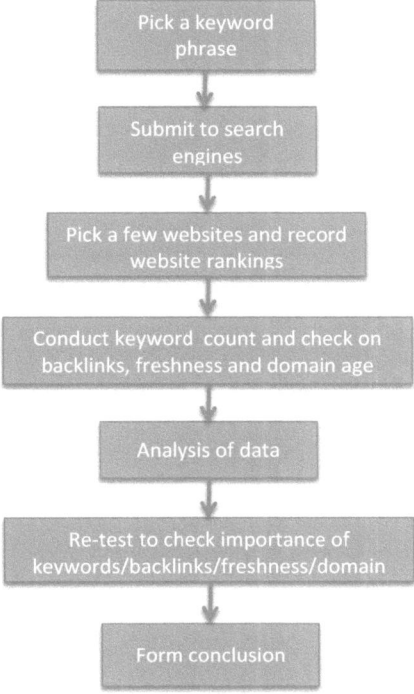

Figure 3.7 Flow chart of test process

CHAPTER 4

4   Data Analysis and Results

4.1 Evaluation of analytic tools

To perform the keyword research the tools to be used need to be accurate. Since most of the tools to be used are available online, a simple analysis will be done to verify the accuracy of the tools using the control website. A target keyword will be used and the result will be compared either manually or by using Google Webmaster Tools and/or Bing Webmaster Tools to verify that the results using the controlled website is correct.

4.1.1 Keyword count analysis using Keyword Density Analyzer

The keyword count for control URL (http://www.transferfactor.com.my/index.htm) using Keyword Density Analyzer tool (http://tools.seobook.com/general/keyword-density/) is shown in Figure 4.1.

Figure 4.1 Snapshot of Keyword Density Analyzer on control website

An actual manual count is performed and the result is then compared with that obtained from the tool as shown in Table 4.1.

Table 4.1 Keyword count results from Keyword Density Analyzer on control website

Keyword Count	Result from tool	Manual counting
Transfer factor	20	20
Transfer factors	14	14

From the above analysis it can be seen that the result from Keyword Density Analyzer is accurate and hence this tool will be used.

4.1.2 Analysis of Inbound Links Using ahrefs

The analysis for inbound links for control URL (http://www.transferfactor.com.my/products.htm) using inbound links checker tool **ahrefs** (https://ahrefs.com/) is shown in Figure 4.2.

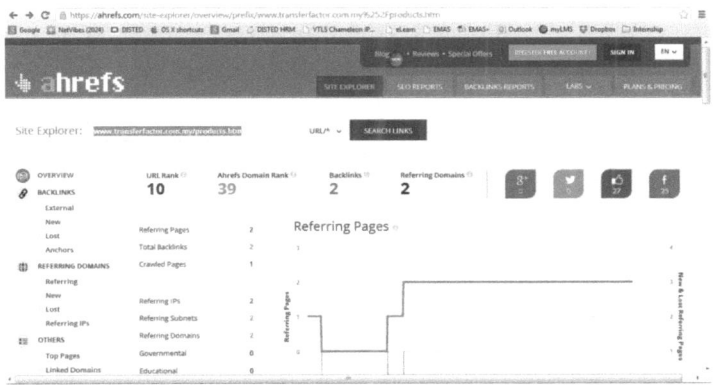

Figure 4.2 Backlinks test results from ahrefs on control website

45

A comparison test is performed using Bing webmaster tools and the result is then compared with that obtained from the tool as shown in Figure 4.3.

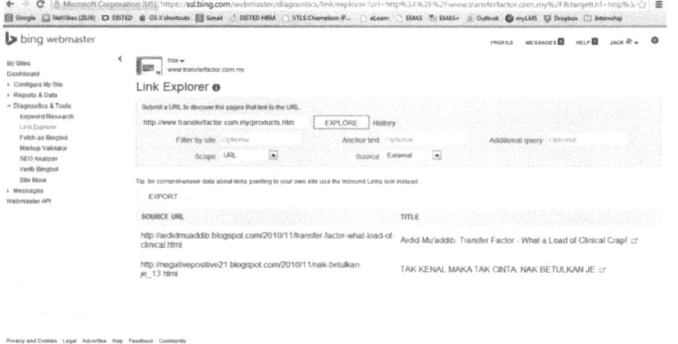

Figure 4.3 Results from Link Explorer in Bing

From the above results it can be seen that both tools show that there are 2 external links to the tested webpage proving that the ahref tool is accurate.

4.1.3 Analysis of Domain Age Using Domain Age Checker from SEOChat

The age of the controlled domain (http://www.transferfactor.com.my/) is tested using Domain Age Checker tool (http://tools.seochat.com/tools/domain-age/) is shown in Figure 4.4.

Figure 4.4 Result of Domain Age on control website

The result of the Domain Age Check corresponds with the actual domain

registration date for the controlled site which was on 14 July 2009 which is

roughly 4 years and 4 months old, hence proving that this tool is accurate.

4.1.4 Analysis of Site Freshness from SiteBeam

The freshness of the controlled domain (http://www.transferfactor.com.my/) is

tested using SiteBeam (http://sitebeam.net/website-tests/freshness/) is shown in

Figure 4.5.

Figure 4.5 Results from freshness test on control website

A scale of 0 to 10 is used to measure freshness with 10 being a site which is updated almost daily and 0 a site which has not been updated for more than 5 years. The result from Site Beam corresponds correctly with the data from control site.

4.1.5 Analysis of Site Ranking using Rank Checking Tool from SEOCentro

The site ranking for the controlled domain (http://www.transferfactor.com.my/) is tested using Rank Checking Tool and the result is compared with actual tests from Google, Yahoo and Bing. The keyword phrase tested was "transfer factor" and the site to search is www.transferfactor.com.my i.e. the controlled site.

*Figure 4.*6 Result from Site Ranking Test on control website

A similar search was done on the three major search engines for the keyword phrase used and the results as tabulated in Table 4 confirms the accuracy of the tool for all 3 search engines. The search engine listing position when doing an organic search for the keyword on 9 December 2013 is as shown in Table 4.2.

48

Table 4.2 Comparison of results from Rank Checker tool and actual search

	Google	Yahoo	Bing
Rank Checker Results	Not found	4	2
Actual Google search	78	-	-
Actual Yahoo search	-	2	-
Actual Bing search	-	-	2

The result in Table 4.2 shows some differences between the tool and actual search result which could be due to geo-targeting and also may be due to the fact that a .my domain is used which might trigger some search engines (possibly Yahoo and Bing) to narrow the search to particular websites from a certain country. A search using Google.com.my shows that the controlled website is listed as the tenth website which supports this assumption. The Rank Checking tool will hence be used just as a guide and the correct ranking will be done by performing an actual search on Google, Bing and Yahoo.

4.1.6 Summary of Tools Analysis

For reasons of brevity, some tools have also been found to be inaccurate and were removed from this study since the primary objective of this research is not to determine the accuracy of the tools. The results from the above tests show that the tools used are accurate to a certain extent and will be selected for the upcoming tests.

Due to the problem of geo-location, tests will also be done only on websites using top level domains only (e.g. .com or .com.my domains) to prevent geo-targeting from affecting the results. The IP address for location of the test conducted will be recorded to show that all the tests are conducted from the same IP location. Also to narrow the scope for this research only keyword phrase with two words will be tested.

4.2 Keyword Analysis Test 1

TEST 1

Aim:

To check the search result and ranking on the search engines on a general search term consisting of two keywords.

Description:

A search is performed on the three major search engines on the keyword phrase "cancer cure". Two high ranking websites with the same top-level domain names will be taken for comparison by measuring their keywords. A comparison on their other metrics (backlinks, freshness and domain age) will also be made to see if these factors somehow affect the rankings.

Results of Test 1

Date of test: 10 December 2013

Test Location IP address: 61.4.110.238

Search phrase: **cancer cure**

Table 4.3 Ranking results of Test 1

Website	Google Rank	Bing Rank	Yahoo Rank
www.cancertutor.com (A)	1	7	7
www.cancernaturalcure.com (B)	72	6	6

Table 4.4 Test 1 results on keyword count and other search metrics

	Website A	Website B
Keyword count in title for "cancer"	1	2
Keyword count in title for "cure"	0	2
Keyword count in text for "cancer"	295	19
Keyword count in text for "cure"	47	4
Keyword count in text for "cancer+cure"	0	0
Domain Backlinks Count	44,572	410
Site Freshness	9.5	n/a
Domain Age	10 years (2003-06-05)	10 years (2003-06-08)

Observations:

1. Website A was ranked highly by all 3 search engines.

2. Website B was ranked first by Bing and Yahoo but placed 74 by Google.

3. Website A has about 20 times more keywords for "cancer" compared to Website B

4. Website A has about 100 times more backlinks compared to Website B

5. Both sites have similar domain age while site freshness data for Website B is not available (n/a).

Conclusion:

1. Google has placed more importance on keyword count and backlinks compared to Bing and Yahoo.

2. Bing and Yahoo could be sharing the same search engine or algorithm

3. No conclusion can be made on whether site freshness and domain age affects the ranking.

4. No conclusion on why Bing and Yahoo ranks website B higher than A.

5. No conclusion on why Google ranks B so differently from Bing and Yahoo but geo-location is suspected.

4.3 Keyword Analysis Test 2

TEST 2

Aim:

To narrow down the search by using a geographical term to exclude possible geo-targeting by search engines.

Description:

A search is performed on the three major search engines on the keyword phrase "penang food". Three high ranking websites with the same top-level domain names will be taken for comparison by measuring their keywords. A comparison on their other metrics (backlinks, freshness and domain age) will also be made to see if these factors somehow affect the rankings.

Results of Test 2

Date of test: 10 December 2013

Test Location IP address: 61.4.110.238

Search phrase: **penang food**

Table 4.5 Ranking result for Test 2

Website	Google Rank	Bing Rank	Yahoo Rank
www.what2seeonline.com (A)	1	5	5
www.penangfoods.com (B)	Not listed	1	1
www.bestpenangfood.com (C)	4	2	2

Table 4.6 Test 2 result on keyword count and other search metrics

	Website A	Website B	Website C
Keyword count in title for "penang"	1	1	1
Keyword count in title for "food"	1	1	1
Keyword count in text for "penang"	323	7	33
Keyword count in text for "food"	140	27	43
Backlinks Count	97,113 5975	4,105 884	3,977 58
Site Freshness	n/a	8.6	9.3
Domain Age	5 years 2008-10-06	5 years 2008-02-26	1 year 2012-07-15

Observations:

1. Website A ranked 1st by Google but only 5th on Bing and Yahoo.

2. Website B was ranked 1st on Bing and Yahoo but not listed on Google (first 10 pages).

This was later verified as due to geo-targeting of that website to Malaysia whereby it was found to rank 10th on Google.com.my.

3. Website A has roughly about 10 times more keywords for "penang" compared to Website C and even more for B.

4. Website A has roughly about 3.5 times more keywords for "food" compared to Website C and even more for B.

5. Website A has about 25 times more backlinks compared to Website B and C.

6. Both A and B have similar domain age while C is younger.

Conclusion:

1. Google has placed more importance on keyword count and backlinks compared to Bing and Yahoo.

2. Bing and Yahoo could be sharing the same search engine or algorithm

3. Although website C has more keywords than B, website B ranked higher on both Bing and Yahoo, possibly due to more backlinks and also longer age.

4. From tests 1 and 2 it can be seen that Google places more importance on backlinks compared with Bing and Yahoo.

5. Domain age could be affecting Google but not so for Bing and Yahoo.

6. Site freshness does not seem to play a big part in determining ranking.

7. Geo-targeting is still affecting the results of tests being done as can be seen by Website B not being listed by Google.

4.4 Keyword Analysis Test 3

<u>TEST 3</u>

<u>Aim:</u>

To narrow down possible geo-targeting by search engines even further by using local search engine servers and comparing only top level .my sites.

<u>Description:</u>

A search is performed only on Google.com.my search engine on the keyword phrase "engineering diploma". Three .my sites listed will be used for keyword comparison to factor off any other geo-targeting factors on different top level domains. A comparison on their other metrics (backlinks, freshness and domain age) will also be made to see if these factors somehow affect the rankings.

<u>Results of Test 3</u>

Date of test: 10 December 2013

Test Location IP address: 61.4.110.238

Search phrase: **engineering diploma**

Table 4.7 Ranking result for Test 3

Website	Google Rank
http://newinti.edu.my/main/academic_programmes/engineering/diploma-in-mechanical-engineering (A)	1
http://www.segi.edu.my/programme/diploma-in-mechanical-engineering (B)	2
http://www.kbu.edu.my/schools-centres/engineering-computing/ (C)	34

Table 4.8 Test 2 results on keyword count and other search metrics

	Website A	Website B	Website C
Keyword count in title for "engineering"	1	1	1
Keyword count in title for "diploma"	1	1	1
Keyword count in text for "engineering"	38	28	30
Keyword count in text for "diploma"	8	8	11
Domain Backlinks Count	6,572	13,663	9,280
Page Backlinks Count	4	3	38
Site Freshness	n/a	9.9	9.1
Domain Age	5 years 2008-10-30	11 years 2002-06-21	17 years 1996-08-09

Observations:

1. Website A ranked 1st by Google also has the highest number of keywords but difference is not much (10 or less).

2. Website C has a higher number of keywords compared to B but is ranked much lower by Google which shows that keyword count is not the only factor affecting ranking.

3. Website B has double the backlinks compared to A but still ranked lower than A which also shows that backlinks are not the sole deciding factor.

4. Website C is much older but still also ranked 30 places lower than A and B by Google which shows that domain age does not count much for ranking.

5. Although A has only 8 to 10 keywords more than B and C it has comparatively less backlinks and is also a newer domain compared to B and C. Site freshness data for A is not available but the site freshness for B and C

are also very high. From here it is suspected another major factor could be the deciding factor to push website A to the top on Google.

Conclusion:

1. Although Website A was ranked highest by Google the ranking progression does not reflect the number of keywords for B and C.
2. Factors like backlinks, freshness and domain age also lean more favorably towards B and C.
3. It is highly possible another major factor is affecting Website A's top performance in Google's ranking system.

4.5 Social Interest Test on Google

TEST 4

Aim:

To check whether social links (e.g. Facebook and Twitter) are affecting Google's ranking algorithm.

Description:

A check is performed on the three websites from Test 3 to gauge the significance of social interest on the websites in affecting their Google search engine rankings. SiteBeam (www.sitebeam.com) will be used as it has a tool to measure the number of Facebook likes and Tweets.

Results of Test 4

Date of test: 12 December 2013

Test Location IP address: 61.4.110.238

Table 4.9 Social interest score for Test 4

Webpage	Facebook Likes	Twitter Tweets	Overall Score
http://newinti.edu.my/main/academic_programmes/engineering/diploma-in-mechanical-engineering (A)	9105	520	9.1
http://www.segi.edu.my/programme/diploma-in-mechanical-engineering (B)	1165	68	6.4
http://www.kbu.edu.my/schools-centres/engineering-computing/ (C)	235	4	3.1

Observations:

1. The overall score from SiteBeam shows a similar pattern as that from

   Google's ranking.

2. The difference between the score of Website A and C also reflects the 30 rank

   differences between A and C on Google.

Conclusion:

1. Google's ranking is possibly affected by social interest.

4.6 Social Interest Test on Bing and Yahoo

TEST 5

Aim:

To check whether social links (e.g. Facebook and Twitter) are also affecting Bing and

Yahoo's ranking algorithms.

Description:

A similar search as in Test 3 is performed on Bing and Yahoo to see if Bing and Yahoo are also using a similar algorithm as Google to rank their search results

Results of Test 5

Date of test: 12 December 2013

Test Location IP address: 61.4.110.238

Search phrase: **engineering diploma**

Table 4.10 Ranking test result for Test 5

Webpage	Bing Ranking	Yahoo Ranking
http://newinti.edu.my/main/academic_programmes/enginee ring/diploma-in-mechanical-engineering (A)	112	112
http://www.segi.edu.my/programme/diploma-in-mechanical-engineering (B)	68	67
http://www.kbu.edu.my/schools-centres/engineering-computing/ (C)	71	71

Observations:

1. All the three sites ranked quite poorly on Bing and Yahoo compared to on Google with Website A scoring the lowest rank even though it has the highest social interest score.

Conclusion:

1. Since the ranking for all 3 sites are poor it would seem that social interest is not a factor affecting both Bing and Yahoo.

59

4.7 Backlinks Check on Bing and Yahoo

TEST 6

Aim:

To check whether backlinks are the factor affecting Bing and Yahoo's ranking algorithms.

Description:

A backlinks check is conducted on the three websites and the results are as shown in Table 4.11.

Results of Test 6

Date of test: 12 December 2013

Test Location IP address: 61.4.110.238

Search phrase: **engineering diploma**

Table 4.11 Backlinks test result for Test 6

Webpage	Bing Ranking	Yahoo Ranking	Domain Backlinks	Keyword "engineering"
http://www.segi.edu.my/programme/diploma-in-mechanical-engineering (B)	68	67	13,663	28
http://www.kbu.edu.my/schools-centres/engineering-computing/ (C)	71	71	9,280	30
http://newinti.edu.my/main/academic_programmes/engineering/diploma-in-mechanical-engineering (A)	112	112	6,572	38

Observation:

1. The ranking by Bing and Yahoo corresponds towards the number of backlinks.

2. There is no observed relation between keywords count and ranking.

Conclusion:

1. Bing and Yahoo are ranking sites based more on backlinks followed by keywords but this is still inconclusive.

4.8 Keyword vs. backlinks test on Bing and Yahoo

TEST 7

Aim:

To confirm whether keywords or backlinks are the major factor affecting Bing and Yahoo's ranking algorithms.

Description:

A keyword and backlinks test is conducted on the first two results from the same search phrase used in Test 6 and the results are shown in Table 4.12.

Results of Test 7

Date of test: 13 December 2013

Test Location IP address: 61.4.110.238

Search phrase: **engineering diploma**

Table 4.12 Keywords and backlinks test result and comparison for Test 7

Webpage	Bing Ranking	Yahoo Ranking	Domain Backlinks	Keyword "engineering"
http://en.wikipedia.org/wiki/Diploma_in_Engineering	1	1	606mil	29
http://www.mdis.edu.sg/academic-programmes/school-of-engineering/diploma-in-engineering	3	2	26,254	23
Compare with Results from Test 6				
http://www.segi.edu.my/programme/diploma-in-mechanical-engineering	68	67	13,663	28
http://www.kbu.edu.my/schools-centres/engineering-computing/	71	71	9,280	30
http://newinti.edu.my/main/academic_programmes/engineering/diploma-in-mechanical-engineering	112	112	6,572	38

Observation:

1. The ranking by Bing and Yahoo corresponds towards the number of backlinks rather than keywords.

2. There is no observed relation between keywords count and ranking.

Conclusion:

2. Bing and Yahoo are ranking sites based on domain backlinks as a major factor.

4.9 Social interest vs. backlinks test on Google

TEST 8

Aim:

To confirm whether social interest or backlinks are the major factor affecting

Google's ranking algorithm.

Description:

A social interest and backlinks test is conducted on the similar results from the same

search phrase used in Test 6 and the results are shown in Table 14.

Results of Test 8

Date of test: 13 December 2013

Test Location IP address: 61.4.110.238

Search phrase: **engineering diploma**

Table 4.13 Social interest test result for Test 8

Webpage	Facebook Likes	Twitter Tweets	Overall Score
http://newinti.edu.my/main/academic_programme s/engineering/diploma-in-mechanical-engineering	9,105	520	9.1
http://en.wikipedia.org/wiki/Diploma_in_Enginee ring	7,992	475	8.9

A comparison is made between the above results and results from social interest,

domain backlinks and keywords count from Test 3 and Test 7. Results are shown in

Table 4.14.

Table 4.14 Social interest score vs. backlinks vs. keyword count

Webpage	Google Ranking	Social Interest	Domain Backlinks	Keyword "engineering"
http://newinti.edu.my/main/academic_programmes/engineering/diploma-in-mechanical-engineering (A)	1	9.1	6,572	38
http://www.segi.edu.my/programme/diploma-in-mechanical-engineering (B)	2	6.4	13,663	28
http://en.wikipedia.org/wiki/Diploma_in_Engineering (D)	6	8.9	606mil	29
http://www.kbu.edu.my/schools-centres/engineering-computing (C)	34	3.1	9,280	30

Observation:

1. The ranking by Google corresponds more towards social interest rather than the number of backlinks and keywords.

2. There is no observed relation between domain backlinks and ranking.

3. There is no observed relation between keywords and ranking.

4. Website B is ranked higher than D although D has a much higher social interest score which is most probably due to geo-location which can be easily confirmed as B is a local site and Google.com.my was used to search.

Conclusion:

1. Google is ranking sites based on social interest as a major factor

2. Other factors like backlinks and keywords may be affecting Google's ranking algorithm but by a lesser degree.

3. Geo-location will affect the rankings of a Google search as Google will serve up local content suitable to the user's location.

4.10   Analysis of Results

From the eight tests done the results are compiled in Table 4.15 for further analysis. The eight tests are listed and also the individual metric measured. A tick is given if the test conducted shows that the search engine was either affected or not affected by the metric during the test.

Table 4.15 Summary of results from all the tests

	Google					Bing					Yahoo				
	Keyword count	Backlinks	Domain Age	Domain Freshness	Social Interest	Keyword count	Backlinks	Domain Age	Domain Freshness	Social Interest	Keyword count	Backlinks	Domain Age	Domain Freshness	Social Interest
Test 1	●	●				□	□				□	□			
Test 2	●	●	●					●	□				●	□	
Test 3	□	□													
Test 4					●										
Test 5										□					□
Test 6							●					●			
Test 7	□	●					●				□	●			
Test 8		□			●										

● – Contributing factor   □ - Non-contributing factor

4.11   Comparison of Results

From the results in Table 5.1 we can further summarize to show the metrics being used by the three search engines to rank their results. The summary is shown in Table 4.16 with 2 dots (●) indicating a strong effect compared to a single dot and no effect seen if there is no dot. The non-contributing factors (□) are not shown as they are somewhat inconclusive and more tests need to be done to proof that those factors were not

affecting the search results at all.

Table 4.16 Summary of search metrics affecting search ranking

	Google	Bing	Yahoo
Keywords	••		
Backlinks	••	••	••
Domain Age	•	•	•
Freshness			
Social Links	•		

A comparison can also be made with the results obtained by Goel and Yadav (Goel,

2013) as summarized in Figure 4.1, which is showing the graphical results based on

their page level keywords evaluation.

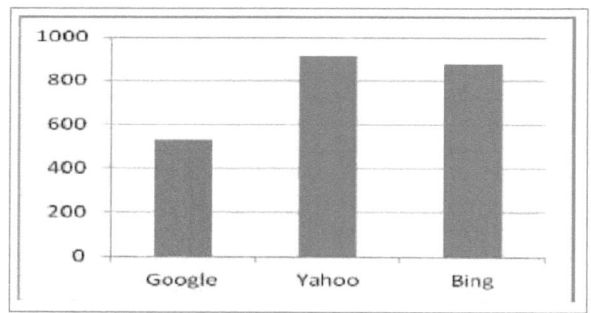

Figure 4.7 Summary of results on page level keywords evaluation (Goel, 2013)

The results of this study does not seem to support the findings of Goel and Yadav

(Goel, 2013) where it was found by them that Yahoo was ranking their sites highest

based on keyword count followed by Bing and Google respectively. This study has

found that it is still possible to rank higher on Yahoo and Bing if keyword count is low

but domain backlinks are high. This research has also found that it is possible to rank higher on Google if keyword count is low but social interest (e.g. links from Facebook and Twitter) are high.

However, the data in this research may not be sufficient enough to support the findings here while Goel and Yadav did their research based on total keywords in the first ten pages of their search results thereby using a much larger corpus of data. Moreover, their research was done by measuring the total number of keywords and the rankings were done based on human ranking. Both researches however seem to be able to find similarities in that Google did not base its rankings on keywords alone.

CHAPTER 5

5   Discussion and Conclusion

5.1 Discussion

This research was basically divided into two parts. The first part involved selecting the

right tools to analyze website properties which may affect their search engine rankings.

The second part was the actual research proper where websites were analyzed based on

their rankings for certain keywords. A control website was set up and used as a

benchmark for some of the tests especially to test the effectiveness of the selected

tools. The tools used in this study were actually preselected as some tools were

discarded when they did not show correct readings for the control website. The reason

for using a control website was to make it possible to judge whether the results

provided by the tools were correct for example the measurement of the age of the

website.

Comparison can also be made using Google Webmaster's Tools

(www.google.com/webmasters/tools/) and Bing Webmaster's Tools

(www.bing.com/toolbox/webmaster) both of which are provided free for the website's

owner in this case the control website. It would be easier if both the tools could be

used for other websites as they have many useful features but alas that was not the case

and therefore the necessity of third party tools to investigate other websites owned by

someone else.

The control website www.transferfactor.com.my had been created in 2009 and so it

was a "safe" website to use as it had been indexed by all the three search engines and hence it would be safe to presume that a search on keywords related to the website will appear as normal as in any organic search and that there is no fear of it having not been indexed yet. Also using Google's and Bing's Webmaster's Tools would easily verify that the website has been indexed.

The other thing about using a control website is the common keywords are well known for this website and this website was also particularly chosen for a targeted keyword phrase – "transfer factor". This phrase was chosen for its uniqueness as it actually consists of two keywords which are quite common and have a meaning of their own but they are quite rarely used as a pair. This particular phrase was also known to occur frequently throughout the website and therefore would ensure that the website will appear in a search on this keyword phrase during the tests. Using an uncommon phrase would also eliminate a lot of other unrelated results during a search and make the top 10 or top 100 search results easier to filter for the websites we are looking for. There are no other reasons for choosing this particular phrase and other randomly selected phrases were also used during the study.

Since there were a lot of third party tools on the internet, this study had preselected the tools to be used for analysis. The effectiveness of the tools were measured using the control website and the tools which failed was removed from this study without any mention as the purpose of this study was not to evaluate the tools and just to use them.

To count the number of keywords in a website the Keyword Density Tool from www.seobook.com was used as it was found to have shown similar readings as that from Google and Bing's Webmaster's Tools. To check the rank of a website the Rank

Checking Tool from www.seocentro.com was used but it was eventually discarded as the rankings were found to be geo-targeted since they were based in the United States. So for the ranking checks actual search on the three search engines were done and the ranks recorded manually. For inbound links test a free tool from ahrefs.com was used after finding it to perform well with the control site. For domain age check the Domain Age Checking Tool from www.seochat.com was used. For site freshness or recent updates check the Site Freshness Tool which was part of a free tool from www.sitebeam.net was used. Finally www.sitebeam.net also provided and analysis of social links which was used to measure social interest on websites under test.

For the actual keywords test, this study used only two-word phrases as this has been found in earlier research (Bilal, 2012) to provide the highest relevant results. The first keyword phrase tested was "**cancer cure**" and it was selected because it is a very common search term for search engines. This first test produced very surprising results as it was seen that the website www.cancertutor.com ranked *first* on Google for the phrase "cancer cure" but only managed to rank *seventh* on Bing and Yahoo. Further evaluation on the first 10 pages of results showed that another website www.cancernaturalcure.com ranked a respectable *sixth* on Bing and Yahoo but only managed to rank *seventy-two* on Google! On analysis, not much can be concluded on why Google ranked the second website so differently from Bing and Yahoo but geo-targeting was suspected as both websites were from the United States. It is suspected that Google was using geo-targeting and decided that the second website was not of much interest to someone in Malaysia while Bing and Yahoo did not employ geo-targeting and assumed the visitor was from the United States. Or it could be the other way around.

Due to the possibility of geo-targeting, the second test was done with a "local flavored" keyword phrase – "**penang food**" to confirm whether geo-targeting was affecting the results. As expected, results were found where a website www.penangfoods.com was ranked *first* on Bing and Yahoo but did not ranked in Google for the first ten pages at all! There could only be two possibilities for this disparity. Either Google banned the website for some reasons or it was again performing geo-targeting as there could not possibly be so much difference in the results from the engines. A check using Google.com.my shows that www.penangfoods.com actually appears on the first page; therefore confirming that it was not banned but geo-targeting was probably in effect.

From the second test it now seems like Bing and Yahoo is performing geo-targeting but Google is not. To solve this problem and to have a level playing field the following tests were then carried out using all three search engines in their local (Malaysian) environment. This was done by accessing all the three search engines locally from http://www.bing.com/?cc=my, http://malaysia.yahoo.com/ and http://google.com.my .

For the third test, all three search engines were accessed locally and again to limit the problem of geo-targeting only sites with Malaysian top level domain names (.my TLD's) were analyzed to level the playing field. The search phrase used was "**engineering diploma**" and the results from three websites with .my TLDs with the highest rankings were evaluated with Google alone. From the results it was seen that the top ranked website had the highest amount of keywords for "engineering". It was also seen that the second ranked website had a slightly lower number of keywords but it had twice the number of backlinks compared to the first website. From here it could be seen that Google does not place much importance on backlinks. However, since the keyword count difference between the top two websites were very small or almost insignificant, it would seem like there are other contributing factors which may cause the first website to rank at the top.

To confirm the assumptions on the third test, the fourth test was then conducted to check social interest factor on the three websites studied in the previous test. It was confirmed in Test 4 that the top ranked website had significantly higher amount of social interest links compared to the other two websites. By now it could be confirmed that Google was ranking websites very much on the social interest scale.

Test 5 was then conducted to see if the three websites in the previous two tests performed similarly on Bing and Yahoo. Bing and Yahoo showed almost similar results but ranked the three websites 112th, 68th and 71st respectively, completely different from Google's rankings (Google ranked them 1st, 2nd and 34th). From here it could be concluded that Bing and Yahoo were not that interested in the social interest factor.

To confirm why Bing and Yahoo ranked the sites as they did, Test 6 was done to check the number of keywords and backlinks for the three websites. The ranking sequence was found to have similarities with the number of domain backlinks pointing back to the domains i.e. the higher the backlinks the higher the rankings. There was no similar pattern found for keyword count. From here it could be observed that Bing and Yahoo were ranking sites based more on backlinks rather than keywords.

Finally, to confirm if backlinks were playing a big part in ranking for Bing and Yahoo, Test 7 was conducted on the same keyword phrase "engineering diploma" and the first two highest ranked websites were measured. Sure enough, although the first two websites did not have .my TLDs they had the highest domain backlinks (606 million, followed by 26,254). The results of this test showed that it was very clear that Bing and Yahoo were ranking websites based on backlinks.

To conclude, a final test was done on Google to measure which of the properties matter most – was it social interest, domain backlinks or keywords. Test 8 showed that Google placed a higher importance on social interest as the sites were ranked almost according to the social interest scale while the effect of backlinks and keyword count did not show any specific relation. While this test showed that Google paid more interest in social interest links it cannot be concluded how much the other factors (including those factors which were not measured) contributed to the ranking. Figure 5.1 shows the combination of factors found in this study to affect Google's rankings.

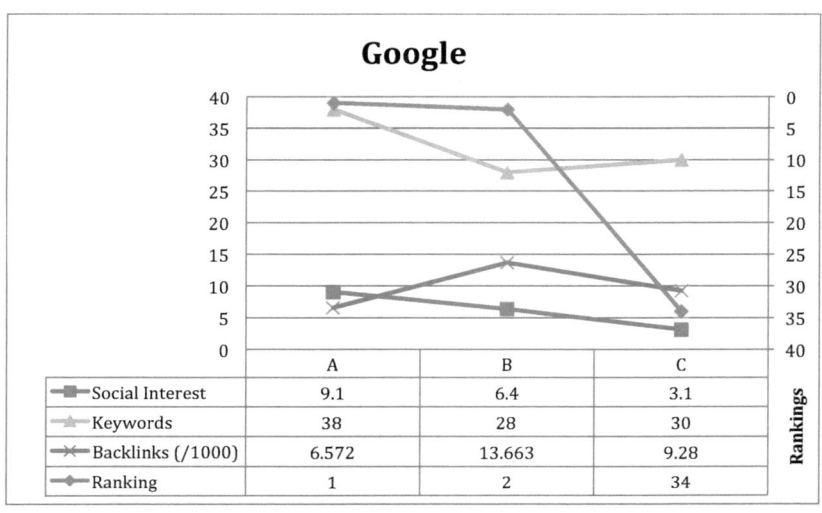

	A	B	C
Social Interest	9.1	6.4	3.1
Keywords	38	28	30
Backlinks (/1000)	6.572	13.663	9.28
Ranking	1	2	34

Figure 5.1 Factors affecting Google's rankings

From the results in this study, we can conclude that Google currently places importance on social interest while the trend for backlinks and keywords are not seen. However this research could not determine the quantum of those search metrics employed.

This study also found that both Bing and Yahoo do not seem to be affected by social interest and their rankings seemed to be more related to backlinks rather than keywords as shown in Figure 5.2 and Figure 5.3.

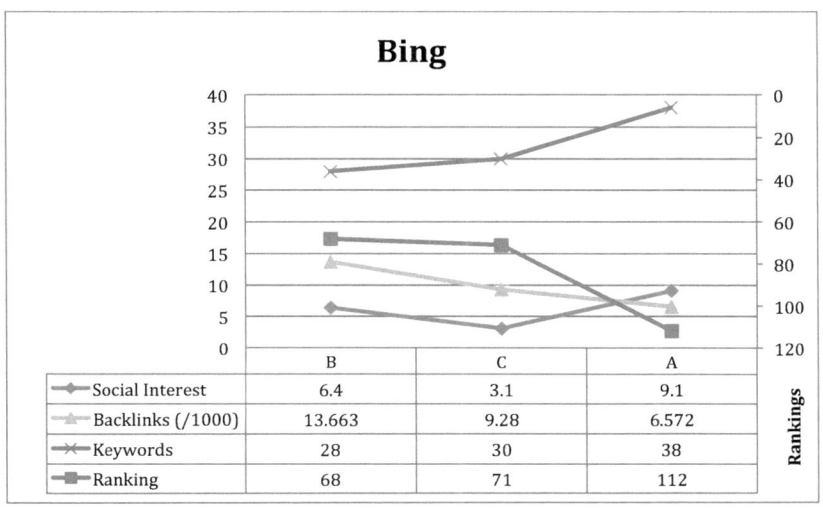

Figure 5.2 Factors affecting Bing's rankings

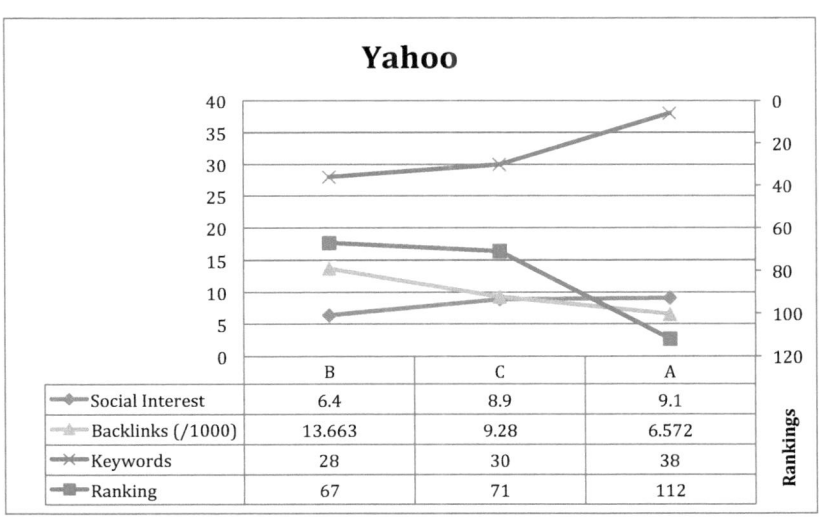

Figure 5.3 Factors affecting Yahoo's rankings

The study also found that data for site freshness were insufficient for a proper analysis but also did not seem to affect the rankings by much while domain age does appear to have some effect on the search results.

From the comparison with related research it can be concluded that Google, Yahoo and Bing do not rely on keywords alone to rank their search results but also various other search metrics such as social interest and backlinks.

5.2 Summary of Findings

The purpose of this research had been to determine whether keywords are a major factor in determining a search result performed on a search engine.

Tests were conducted on the three main search engines being used today namely Google, Bing and Yahoo to see if keywords are still a measure of relevance in a search. The results has shown that although keywords are still being used as a metric for measurement to retrieve results, search engines today use many other factors to determine which result is more relevant and to present the most relevant ones at the top of a search result page. Although keywords are important this research shows that the number of keywords in a webpage does not determine its relevance as webpage with high number of keywords were not ranked above those with lower numbers of keywords.

Bing and Yahoo were found to have placed more importance on backlinks or the number of link-backs to a website as a measure of relevance. Those websites having more backlinks to their domains were placed as more relevant and ranked higher compared with those with less backlinks.

Although Google too placed some importance on backlinks, nevertheless it was found that backlinks did not carry as much weight for Google as they did for Bing and Yahoo. Google was found to include social interest as one of the factors to measure relevance and websites with higher social interest were ranked higher than those with lesser social interest. In contrast social interest did not affect the rankings of Bing and Yahoo at all.

5.3 Limitations

This research was done only on two keywords phrase. Although this managed to shorten the time of the research it did not manage to reveal what would happen if a longer or shorter phrase was used. Two keywords phrase were chosen as research shows two keywords are the second most common number of keywords after single keywords ("Keyword and Search Engines Statistics," 2013) while a single keyword would have increased the number of search results thereby complicating the research.

This research was also limited to only one location to minimize problem of redundant servers which may serve up different results of a search if different servers were accessed. However it cannot be ruled out those redundant servers may still have affected the results although all tests were done at a single location as there was no monitoring of which search engine server was being used during each test.

The other factor which was affecting the results was the geo-location factor whereby a search engine will narrow down the result of a search based on either the location of the user or whether the user is using the local variant of a search engine. Geo-location is actually a good feature of a search engine as search engines become more intelligent and try to serve up results suited more for the user at its present location. However in this research it sometimes poses as an additional factor which may cloud the results if two search engines were tested at the same time without knowing whether they were using geo-location or not. A search engine using geo-location will serve up more local results compared with another one which does not and this will affect the comparison of rankings.

5.4 Conclusion

This research has shown that keywords are no longer the main factor a search engine will use to determine the results of a search. Factors such as backlinks play a big role as a measurement of relevance for search engines like Bing and Yahoo which is basically more directory based search engines. This research has also shown that Google is now measuring social interest on a website as a measure of its relevance and websites which have acquired a large social following will be ranked higher.

5.5 Future research recommendations

This research has shown that if you want to search for a site based on keywords and references then Bing or Yahoo should be your choice of search engine. However if you want to search for a site which is popular then Google should be your choice as it measures social interest as one of the relevant factors in a search. However since Google is now the de facto search engine with the most users, almost every internet marketer would want its website being listed highly on Google. However, social interest is not the only other factor as Google places importance also on factors like site authority and quality links. It is therefore recommended that any future research be done to find out how these two factors are being measured by Google.

On research for keywords more work could be done to find out if the actual location of keywords in text body area, meta tags, title tags and even the URL itself are also affecting the result of a search.

It is also interesting to note that while Google placed a lot of importance on social links neither Bing nor Yahoo ranked their websites based on social interest. This raise a question as to whether it is reasonable for Google to placed such an amount of importance on social interest bearing in mind that social links only came to the picture not so long ago. Is social interest really a measure of a website's relevance?

It would also seems like Google is now defining which website is relevant and which is not, using its own rules and the people who use Google are relying on Google and eventually trusting Google to give them the right website and the right answer. However, the rules which Google are using are not made known to the public and even the SEO professionals are guessing at best on what rules Google are using to rank websites.

On hindsight it looks like after all these years no one is exactly sure how websites should be ranked or are being ranked according to their relevance while almost everyone trusts Google outright to give them the correct results. Google is also changing their algorithm almost every year and every time the algorithm is changed, all developers have to relook their websites again to check if they have fallen off Google's radar. An immediate drop in traffic and a sudden loss of income generated from the internet usually is a sign that Google has dropped your website's ranking.

It can also be seen on Google recently that it is now heavily relying on "authority" whereby websites which have known authors and especially those with Google+ accounts are being more prominently featured. This evidently also raises a question as to whether Google is unfairly using the internet to promote its own social network and raises doubts on how Google is measuring "authority" and whether proper research has been done to justify whether such authority contributes to relevance in a search.

A website's relevance to a search should be based on properly researched metrics but to a casual web user a search ultimately begins with a keyword(s) entry. For this reason it is still logical to presume that keyword research will still be a mainstay for a search engine to perform a search for many years to come.

Bibliography

Agostini, A. (2011). Search engine optimization and international branding. *Multilingual*, 22(1), 45-49.

Barsky, E., & Bar-Ilan, J. (2012). The impact of task phrasing on the choice of search keywords and on the search process and success. *Journal Of The American Society For Information Science & Technology, 63*(10), 1987-2005. doi:10.1002/asi.22654

Bilal, D. (2012). Ranking, relevance judgment, and precision of information retrieval on children's queries: Evaluation of Google, Yahoo!, Bing, Yahoo! Kids, and ask Kids. *Journal of the American Society for Information Science & Technology, 63*(9), 1879-1896. doi: 10.1002/asi.22675

Brin S., Page L. (1998): The Anatomy of a Large-Scale Hyper textual Web Search Engine. *Proceedings of 7th International World Wide Web Conference, pages 107–117.*

Brin S., Page L., Motwani R., Winograd T. (1999): The pagerank citation ranking: Bringing order to the web. *Technical report, Stanford Digital Libraries SIDL-WP, pp. 1999-0120.*

Dover, D. and E. Dafforn (2011). *Secrets : Search Engine Optimization (SEO) Secrets.* Hoboken, NJ, USA, Wiley.

Geographical Targeting. (2013).   Retrieved 1 December 2013, from https://developers.google.com/adwords/api/docs/appendix/geotargeting?csw=1

Gerace, T. (2013). How to Catch a Hummingbird: Benefitting from Google's New Algorithm.   Retrieved 1 November 2013, from http://socialmediatoday.com/tgerace/1833761/how-catch-hummingbird-benefitting-googles-new-algorithm

Ledford, Jerry L. (2008). SEO: *Search Engine Optimization Bible.* Indianapolis, IN, USA, Wiley.

Meng, X., & Xing, S. (2005). *Search Engine Comparison Performance.* Manuscript, submitted for publication. September 2005.

Malaga, R. A. (2009). WEB 2.0 TECHNIQUES FOR SEARCH ENGINE OPTIMIZATION: TWO CASE STUDIES. *Review of Business Research, 9*(1), 132-139.

Palanisamy, R. (2013). Evaluation of Search Engines: A Conceptual Model and Research Issues. *International Journal of Business & Management, 8*(6), 1-15. doi:10.5539/ijbm.v8n6p1

ROUSSINOV, D., WEIGUO, F., & ROBLES-FLORES, J. (2008). Beyond Keywords: Automated Question Answering on the Web. *Communications of the ACM, 51*(9), 60-65.

SHALYA, N., SHUKLA, S., & ARORA, D. (2012). An Effective Content Based Web Page Ranking Approach. *International Journal of Engineering Science & Technology, 4*(8), 3876-3880.

Search Engine Ranking Factors. (2013).   Retrieved 1 November 2013, from http://moz.com/search-ranking-factors.

Zhao, L. (2004). Jump Higher: Analyzing Web-Site Rank in Google. *Information Technology & Libraries, 23*(3), 108-118.

References

Agarwal, A. (2007). How To See Google Results of Another Country or City from Your
Location.   Retrieved 1 December 2013, from
http://www.labnol.org/internet/search/how-to-see-google-results-of-another-
country-or-city-from-your-location/1206/

Anderson, S. (2009). What Is The IDEAL Keyword Density Percentage?   Retrieved 1
November 2013, from http://www.hobo-web.co.uk/keyword-density-seo-myth/

Bilal, D. (2012). Ranking, relevance judgment, and precision of information retrieval on
children's queries: Evaluation of Google, Yahoo!, Bing, Yahoo! Kids, and ask
Kids. *Journal Of The American Society For Information Science & Technology*,
63(9), 1879-1896. doi:10.1002/asi.22675

comScore Releases July 2013 U.S. Search Engine Rankings. (AUGUST 14, 2013).
Retrieved 1 November 2013, from
http://www.comscore.com/Insights/Press_Releases/2013/8/comScore_Releases_J
uly_2013_U.S._Search_Engine_Rankings

Couzin, G. and Grappone, J. (2008). *Search Engine Optimization An Hour A Day*, 2nd
Edition. Hoboken, NJ, USA, Wiley.

Dover, D., & Dafforn, E. (2011). *Secrets : Search Engine Optimization (SEO) Secrets*. Hoboken, NJ, USA: Wiley.

Fishkin, R. (2013). A Visual Guide to Keyword Targeting and On-Page Optimization Retrieved 1 November 2013, from http://moz.com/blog/visual-guide-to-keyword-targeting-onpage-optimization

Geetha, S., & Sathiyakumari, K. (2012). LINK PREDICTION MODEL FOR PAGE RANKING OF BLOGS. *International Journal on Computer Science & Engineering, 4*(11), 1854-1862.

Goel, S. a. Y., S. (2013). Search Engine Evaluation Base on Page Level Keywords. *IEEE International Advance Computing Conference (IACC)*.

How Does Google Collect and Rank Results. (10 January 2006). Retrieved 15 October 2013, from http://www.free-seo-news.com/newsletter194.htm

Jones, K. B. (2008). *Search Engine Optimization : Your Visual Blueprint to Effective Internet Marketing*. Hoboken, NJ, USA, Visual.

Keyword and Search Engines Statistics. (2013). Retrieved 15 October 2013, from http://www.keyworddiscovery.com/keyword-stats.html

Kim, L. Internet Search Engines History. Retrieved 1 October 2013, from http://www.wordstream.com/articles/internet-search-engines-history

Miller, M. (2012, August 13, 2012). Geolocation Changes Google Keyword Rankings 69% of Time. Retrieved 1 November 2013, from http://searchenginewatch.com/article/2198253/Geolocation-Changes-Google-Keyword-Rankings-69-of-Time-Report

The Periodic Table Of SEO Success Factors. Retrieved 1/11/2013, from http://searchengineland.com/seotable

Sharma, D. K., & Sharma, A. K. (2010). A Comparative Analysis of Web Page Ranking Algorithms. *International Journal on Computer Science & Engineering*, 2670-2676.

Sullivan, D. (Sep 17, 2010). Schmidt: Listing Google's 200 Ranking Factors Would Reveal Business Secrets. Retrieved 1 November 2013, from http://searchengineland.com/schmidt-listing-googles-200-ranking-factors-would-reveal-business-secrets-51065

Sullivan, D. (Sep 26, 2013). FAQ: All About The New Google "Hummingbird" Algorithm. Retrieved 1 November 2013, from http://searchengineland.com/google-hummingbird-172816

Witten, I. H., Gori, M., & Numerico, T. (2007). *Web Dragons : Inside the Myths of Search Engine Technology*. Burlington, MA, USA: Morgan Kaufmann.